DIARY OF ONE
WHO VANISHED

DIARY OF ONE
WHO VANISHED

A SONG CYCLE BY Leoš Janáček

OF POEMS BY Ozef Kalda

IN A NEW VERSION BY

Seamus Heaney

FARRAR, STRAUS AND GIROUX
NEW YORK

cop.1

Farrar, Straus and Giroux
19 Union Square West, New York 10003

Printed in the United States of America
Designed by Holly McNeely
First published in 1999 by Faber and Faber Ltd., Great Britain
First published in the United States by Farrar, Straus and Giroux
First American edition, 2000

Library of Congress Cataloging-in-Publication Data
Janáček, Leoš 1854–1928.
    [Zápisník zmizelého. Text. English]
    Diary of one who vanished : a song cycle / by Leoš Janáček ;
in a new version by Seamus Heaney.
       p.   cm.
    Poems originally written by Ozef Kalda and published
anonymously around 1917, set into a song cycle by Janáček,
here put into a new English version of the poems by Heaney.
    ISBN 0-374-13923-7 (alk. paper)
    1. Song cycles—Texts. I. Heaney, Seamus. II. Kalda, Ozef.
    III. Title.

ML54.2.Z36 J32 2000
782.4′7—dc21

                                        00-024266

INTRODUCTION

In the summer of 1917, the composer Leoš Janáček went for his usual holiday to the Moravian spa town of Luhačovice. It was his custom to spend a few weeks on his own there every year, taking the waters and going for long walks. He was sixty-three, finally coming into his own as an artist of classic stature, and in the next decade his creative powers would crest even more abundantly.

This late flowering was inspired to a great extent by his meeting during that July in Luhačovice with a young married woman called Kamila Stösslová. John Tyrrell's edition of the correspondence that ensued (*Intimate Letters: Leoš Janáček to Kamila Stösslová*, Faber, 1994) gives an extraordinarily detailed and revealing account of how the relationship with Kamila developed and kept the ever-susceptible composer obsessed and busy. A year after their first encounter, Janáček was writing to her from his home village of Hukvaldy:

> I work from time to time and in the evening I sit beneath my lime tree and gaze into the forest until the night envelops it. Silence goes to sleep under every tree. The cock wakes me in the morning. He "sings" such a strange melody that I haven't yet been able to notate it.

Janáček was then engaged upon the work that would eventually appear as *Diary of One Who Vanished*, and it is impossible not to connect the sense of place and expectancy that come through in the above passage with the greenwood setting, the mixture of stealth and transport, in the songs as we now have them.

These are settings of a sequence of poems which

the composer had encountered the previous year in *Lidové noviny* (People's Paper), a daily published in the town of Brno, where Janáček lived and taught. The poems have recently been identified as the work of Ozef Kalda, but they first appeared "From the Pen of a Self-Taught Man" and told a story of sexual infatuation, a dark-eyed gypsy and a haunted farmer's boy, the standard fare of folk song. When, however, Kamila entered the field of musical force, a personal intensity began to give power from below the surface. Inside a month, Janáček was telling her:

> Regularly in the afternoon a few motifs occur to me for those beautiful little poems about that Gypsy love. Perhaps a nice little musical romance will come out of it—and a tiny bit of the Luhačovice mood would be in it.

And in September of the following year, when he was having difficulty finishing the work, hurt at Kamila's not having replied to his recent letters, he further identified her with the "Zefka" of the poems: "It's too bad my Gypsy girl can't be called something like Kamilka. That's why I also don't want to go on with the piece."

In my versions of the poems, I call Janik "Johnny," simply because the English diminutive of John is nicely and rightly poised between term of endearment and country vernacular; for similar reasons, I call fledglings "scaldies" and the tree in the hedge a "boor tree"—an Ulster Scots term which I like to think eroticizes the elder as a "bower tree." But Zefka remains Zefka, the oxen remain oxen, and roosters still crow in these lines as they did in the original, because for all the Moravian (or Ulster) local colour, the true setting of the events recounted in *Diary of One Who Vanished* is the clear and passionate land of "once upon a time." And for all the poems' dependence upon the cadences of the Wallachian dialect, which appealed to Janáček because it resembled the rural speech of his childhood, their ultimate home was to be in the new country of melody and desire. The familiar cadences were like a childhood sweetheart with whom the composer fleetly and sweetly eloped.

The job of making a new singable translation began as an experiment, but in the course of the preliminary meetings with Deborah Warner, Ruby Philogene, Ian Bostridge, and Julius Drake, it became an excitement and an education. I had started by listening to recordings of the work in Czech, then trying to get words that kept close to the meanings but retained an English "sound of sense" and a certain metrical feel. At our first working session, however, the fine tuning began, the trading of rhymes and syllables, the give of speech and the take of song. I was indeed lucky to be introduced to the ancient lyric discipline of fitting words to music in such perfectly pitched (and jocund) company.

S.H.

DIARY OF ONE
WHO VANISHED

FIRST PERFORMED BY THE
ENGLISH NATIONAL OPERA
Ian Bostridge, Young Man
Ruby Philogene, Gypsy
Chorus
Pianist: Julius Drake
Director: Deborah Warner
Designers: Jean Kalman and Tom Pye
Costume Designer: John Bright

IRISH PREMIERE
Gaiety Theatre
Dublin
15 October 1999

BRITISH PREMIERE
Lyttleton Theatre
Royal National Theatre
London
4 November 1999

I

I startled this young gypsy girl
Lightfooted as a deer,
Black ringlets on her mushroom breast,
Her eyes like the night air,
Two eyes that cut deep into me
As she slipped behind a tree,
Two eyes that haunt and follow me
All the long

        long day.

II

That dark gypsy lass
Keeps coming to the townland:
Why is she still out there?
Why is she still out there?
What brings her near the place?

My heart, be still and wait.
Pray God grant me respite
And pray that praying helps
Or my plight is helpless.

III

Glow-worms in the gloaming
Glimmer through their dances,
In the twilit hay-field
A lonely figure wanders.

Keep away. Leave me be
For I won't be tempted.
Why do I see so clear
Mother brokenhearted?

Now the moon is setting,
Country shadows darken:
Someone stands stock-still
Beyond there, past the gable.

Two eyes like hot coals

Are glowing in the night.

God Almighty, O dear

God Almighty, help me!

Send me Your light.

IV 🗡

Now small scaldies twitter
And chirrup in their nest.
I have lain awake all night
As if on thistles.

Now it is break of day,
The east fills up with dawn.
I have lain awake all night
On a bed of thorn!

V

Ploughing makes me weary,
I got so little sleep
And when I did get sleep
Dreaming of her woke me.

VI 🗡

Top it up, my oxen team,

And plough it straight and take the strain.

Don't look near the boor-tree hedge,

Just top it up and plough it down.

Ploughshare bumps off ground that's hard

And everything is skid and kick.

Flutter of a headscarf frill,

Shadow-dapple, hide-and-seek.

Who's out there

                haunting me

I want her

                turned to stone.

Throbbing head.

                Molten lead

Is pouring through

                my burning mind.

VII ✒

My plough-pin is broken.
I'll have to stop and mend it.
So, oxen, stand your ground,
Soon all will work again.

Over there I'll cut one
From that boor-tree bower.
Who can escape his fate?
Fate comes upon its hour.

VIII ✒

You oxen, don't be sad.

Don't be afraid to look.

Don't be afraid, I say.

I'll come back from the wood.

Dark-haired Zefka stands there

In the deep boor-tree shade.

Night-sparkle from a fire

The brilliance of her gaze.

Don't be afraid, I say.

Even though she is there—

Shifting shape—

I'll resist

Her hide-

and-seek allure.

IX ❧

"Johnny, you are welcome
Underneath the greenwood.
What star kept you on course,
Well and truly guided?

"Johnny, you are welcome!
What are you afraid of?
You are pale, you are scared.
Are you scared of me, love?"

"Scared? Why should I scare from
You or from anyone?
I'm here to cut and wedge
And whittle sharp a pin."

"O Johnny, there's no need
To whittle and sharpen.
I'll sing. Listen now.
Hear my gypsy song now."

THREE WOMEN (offstage in low voices)

Then she joined her hands
Singing her sad hurt
And the notes she sang
Ravished his young heart.

X ✒

God Almighty, hidden from us,
Why did You give gypsies life?
Coming, going, toing, froing,
Moved along and hunted off.

"Can you hear larks, Johnny,
The skylarks rising there?"

THREE WOMEN

And the notes she sang
Ravished his young heart.

"Sit and rest, be happy
Beside a gypsy girl.

"God Almighty, God of mercy,
Grant, grant me this
Before I leave this world:
Let me near life,
Let me know it."

THREE WOMEN

And the notes she sang
Ravished his sad heart.

"Still you stand there staring,

Silent as a statue.

Do I scare you that much?

What has happened to you?

Move beside me closer.

Why are you so distant?

Is it just my colour?

Does that still disturb you?

My face and hands and arms

Are burnt dark in the sun

But parts I'll let you see

The sunlight's never seen."

THREE WOMEN

She opened her blouse,
She showed her unsunned self,

His young blood was rising,

His young blood was rising.

XI 🦋

Fragrance fills the woodland,
Wind-swayed wheat is ripe.
"Now, Johnny, I'll show you
How sunburnt gypsies sleep."
With that she broke a branch
And laid it on a stone:
"There now, my bed is made,"
She lightly said, and laughed.
"Earth is my pillow,
The sky my counterpane.

I keep my dew-cold fingers

Warm-buried in my lap."

In her skirt she lay

Bare on the barren ground

And for sad virtue's sake

He wept with a sad heart.

XII ✒

Dappled woodland light,
Spring well chill and bright,
Eyes like stars at night,
Open knees so white.
Four things death itself won't cover,
Unforgettable forever.

XIII ✎

[*Piano solo: Andante*]

XIV ✎

Sun and sunlight heighten,
Shadows shorten.
Who, O who can bring back
All I have forfeited?

XV ✭

Move, you tawny oxen!
What are you looking at?
Could it be you're waiting
To let my secret out?
Try it and you'll see
The flogging I'll give you.
Just you try, my oxen,
Then see what will happen!

Now I dread my summons,
The noonday Angelus
That calls me home, alas,
To meet my mother's eyes.

XVI ✈

How did this happen me?
Can I live to bear it?
And take this girl to wife?
And rear a gypsy brat?
Gypsies all around me,
Father, mother? Never!

O find a millstone quickly!
Throw me in the millrace!
Even skylarks singing
Unearthly melodies
Cannot ease this sadness
Or bring joy to my days.

XVII ✒

Who can escape his fate?
Fate comes upon its hour.
Evenings now I hurry
To the boor-tree bower.
What is it leads me there?
Looking for strawberries . . .
Tiny leaves prinked open.
Taste of felicity!

XVIII ✒

Night-time, night-time, night-time
Cannot come soon enough,
Dark night in Zefka's bed,
The small hours of love.
Roosters, I'll wring your necks
If you don't stop crowing.
Roosters, your cry at dawn
Is beyond enduring—
Interrupting love's
Deep dream and yearning.
With her in my arms
I defy the morning.

XIX ✏

Magpie, sorrow's magpie
Rising up suddenly,
Did you rob my sister's
Washing on wash day?
What if she should ever
Find who the real thief was?
She would abhor me,
All of my lies to her.

Holy God, Holy God,
What has come over me?
Everything's upended. God,
What has happened to me?

I kick against myself

Like a horse that's spancelled.

Prayers pour through my mind like

Sand down through an hourglass.

XX 🕊

Now she's in full bloom

How she ti- ti- tightens dresses!

Now her time has come

Look how bri- bri- bright-eyed she is!

XXI

Father, what made you think
My match could be arranged?
Father, you little knew
What sort of son you'd raised.
As the night follows day
Punishment's sure to come.
Father, my fate is clear,
Cannot be escaped from.

XXII ✍

Fare you well, my townland,

Fare you well, my people.

Nothing matters here now.

I embrace my exile.

So farewell, Father dear,

And farewell, my Mother.

Fare you well, Sister dear,

Farewell, my little flower.

Pardon me, don't blame me,

Take my hand and kiss it.

cop·l

There'll be no returning.

To find my life, I lose it.

Destiny directs me.

Life's doorway stands open.

Zefka waits and calls me,

Nursing our firstborn son.